André Mangeot is a professional charity fundraiser who lives and works near Cambridge. His short stories have appeared in *London Magazine* and his poetry in many British and American journals. In recent years he has won prizes in the Yorkshire, Kent & Sussex and Bridport competitions and been shortlisted for the Blackwells/TLS prize.

He is a member of the performance group Joy of Six which has played at venues across England and in New York.

A short book of poems, *Natural Causes*, was published by Shoestring Press in 2003. *Mixer* is his first full-length collection.

Mixer

André Mangeot

NORWICH

Egg Box Publishing
25 Brian Avenue, Norwich, NR1 2PH

The Egg Box Web Site Address is:
newwriting.net

The Joy of Six Web Site Address is:
joyofsix.co.uk

First Published in Great Britain by
Egg Box Publishing, 2005

Copyright © André Mangeot, 2005

The author asserts the moral right to be
identified as the author of this work

ISBN 0-9543920-4-3

Printed and bound in Great Britain by
Biddles, King's Lynn

All rights reserved. No part of this publication may be reproduced,
stored in a retrieval system, or transmitted in any form or by
any means, electronic, mechanical, photocopying, recording
or otherwise, without the prior permission of the publishers.

This book is sold subject to the condition that it shall not, by way
of trade or otherwise, be lent, re-sold, hired out or otherwise
circulated without the publisher's prior consent in any form of
binding or cover other than that in which it is published and
without a similar condition including this condition being
imposed on the subsequent purchaser.

Designed by Alexander Gordon Smith

For Colin Byrne and Mark Boswell
in continuing friendship –
and for Roslyn, with all my heart.

Mixer /míksər/ noun

1. A person who blends or mixes liquids, materials, etc; spec. a person who mixes drinks, a bartender.
2. A machine or device for mixing; a container for mixing drinks; a cocktail-shaker.
3. A person in respect of his or her ability to mix socially with others; a sociable person.
4. A soft drink with which an alcoholic drink is diluted, as soda water etc; an alcoholic drink used in cocktails.
5. A trouble maker.

M I X E R

ONE

Atta Boy 12

Blood & Sand 13

Welcome, Stranger 15

Fallen Angel 16

Alaska 18

Daily Mail 20

Clap of Thunder 21

Amsterdam 23

Tornado 24

TWO

AWOL 28

Starboard Light 30

Zipper 31

Bull Dog 33

Great Secret 34

Novocaine 36

Green Room 37

Scotch Mist 38

THREE

Brainstorm 42

Garryowen 43

Alexei's Sister 45

Dunlop 47

A Fine Balance 48

Pete 50

Southern Belle 51

Sanctuary 53

M I X E R

Four	**Five**	**Six**
Babies 56	Firebird 76	Affinity 86
Sunset 57	Crossbow 79	Beam Me Up Scotty 87
Henry's Last Hurrah 58	Upstairs 80	
Smokey 61	Summer Rain 83	
S.W.1 62		
Slipstream 63		
Wobbly Knee 64		
Cowboy 66		
Thistle 68		
Deep Sea 69		
Ward Eight 70		
Ceasefire 72		

"The **problem** with the **world** is that **everyone** is a **few drinks** behind."

Humphrey Bogart

Atta Boy

7ml French Vermouth
53ml Dry Gin
4ds Grenadine

Shake & strain

Don't say you're surprised –
where else would I feel as at home? –
me with a name for mixing it, always one
for the crowd, the chatter, the glint in her eye
and never averse
to a bite of the juice?

But this hour, the quietest,
is almost the best – clocking on,
walking in, place to myself, flicking the switch
to a still-polished gleam of counter and rail,
glasses and optics, bar mirror
doubling my little nirvana.

                Dan hustles in, off-loading a jacket.
Checks his reflection, three buttons open.
Tugs at his gel. *Some fair stuff outside …*
be wicked tonight. With a minute to go
                we high-five it, he heads for the door,
bends to unlock. They're already

massing – vaporous shadows
behind the smoked glass. *Ready to jive?*
Patrolling our long narrow trench I salute him, steeled
for the surge to our lines.
Lay hands on the bar. Await
the first shot.

Blood & Sand

20ml Orange Juice
20ml Sweet Vermouth
20ml Scotch Whisky
20ml Cherry Brandy

Shake & strain

It was all I saw her drink – the only one
she wanted, as she wanted him. Through the din,
the ringing tills, working there beside him you could sense
his focus on the door. Each time she floated in

(a year back, give or take) he'd have the speedrail
and the sweet-talk primed, catch her eye
and draw her to the bar. She'd lean in close and laugh –
then watch him work that shaker for his very life.

Maya. And who could argue? Picasso-curved,
a mane of pitch, anthropology at LSE. A babe.
He had her number that first night – and she had his.
Ah, my Ben, she'd coo, *mi toro cariñoso* – in such a way

I shivered even then. Recalled the only bullfight
I have seen: Majorca, long ago, a cheap and grisly thrill –
the fooling and the toying, the ribboned darts, the sword
secreted in the swirl of cape and cheers before the kill

while he, of course, just strutted, centre-stage, his grin
a counter-wide. Wouldn't hear a word against, even had I
guts to try. *She's ... I can't tell you, man* (by now he'd
clock in hazy, late, a shadow) and I thought *that's fine* –

I'd heard already what her tongue could do, how Toledo
was the place, why she worshipped Hemingway. Bit my lip
as he grew pale, lost touch and weight, left the rest of us
to field each slip of change, forgotten order, half-arsed shift.

One night she simply wasn't there. Smile and swagger gone,
from then he never spoke of her. I couldn't leave it anymore:
our free day, Monday, grabbed some beer and takeaway –
drove over to his flat, walked in the open door

and there he was, man of action – slumped out in a chair,
book upon his chest, ringed by empties. Like a cape
just whipped aside, the poster of the matador had gone –
its outline left in dust, ripped plaster, Sellotape –

the bookshelves, too, were bare, the failing light outside
leaching each last drop of colour from the room.
I went through to the kitchen, set to on the dishes. Let him sleep,
that paper shield across his chest. *Death in the Afternoon.*

Welcome, Stranger

12ml Grenadine
12ml Lemon Juice
12ml Orange Juice
12ml Dry Gin
12ml Rum Appleton
12ml Brandy

Shake & strain

When she woke up saying
I could murder a beer,
the pint-sized dancer
who'd never touched booze
but whose freshly-stitched chest
now beat with the ticker
of a Harrogate bouncer

when the guy who had held
every chauvinist view,
but newly plugged in
to the strait-laced heart
of a primary-school teacher
now lay down his paper
and smiled open-faced
as his wife had her say

both scientists and surgeons
were stumped for an answer,
went scurrying back
to their notes on the donors

while two bemused partners
wondered just where and how
their soulmates had gone –
who it was they were holding,
kissing, sleeping with now.

Fallen Angel

53ml Gin
7ml Fresh Lemon or Lime Juice
2ds Crème de Menthe
ds Angostura

Shake & strain

Then I opened the paper and there you were –
someone I'd last seen in college, back in the 70's

a brilliant guy, Indian, born with the gift of the word –
ace of debaters, producer of plays, of dazzling

original essays, holding court with a glass
or poem in hand, resplendent in scarf or cravat

eyes blazing, tongue racing with tumbling insight.
And of course we envied the attention you drew

how you managed it all without effort while we
struggled on, print swimming and blurring

late through the night for a panload of nothing.
Even later, drifting quickly apart, your brilliance

shadowed us still from faraway places, getting there
first with the prizes, books published, travelling

fellowships, sun that we craved, and now here they are
those same gimlet eyes staring back from the page,

around you, as ever, words and more words,
your war with the darkness behind all the glitter –

all coming down to a day in Toronto, the Library,
ten final letters penned at white heat, one short drive

to the Bloor St Viaduct to stretch out your arms –
fly like the comet I remember, out across the night sky.

Alaska

50ml Dry Gin
12ml Chartreuse

Shake & strain

It was either this, you said, or a three-year stretch
in Riyadh, Jeddah – magicking the latest palace,
mosque or golf-links from the sand – anything to fix
a life derailed by botched affairs, by alimony, lawyers,
the business sold from under you, the self-destruction
of a self-made man. But what propelled you on that flight
to Fairbanks (other than the Trans-Alaska pipeline and your
welder's skill, the prospect of a hundred-grand to start again
just two years down the line) was snow and ice, those continents
of emptiness that first distracted you on globes, in atlases –
the lure of Eskimos and ice-floes, grizzlies, permafrost,
months of winter dark, the northern lights. So you made it
to the Union Hall, signed up, waited daily till they bussed you
up the Haul Road with a load of oilers, bullcooks, engineers –
across Brooks Range, the Yukon into Tulik camp. And there
it all began: rigged out in muklaks, blowtorch, spark-mask –
twelve hours on, twelve for chow and sleep; overtime
and bonuses for crews completing ten miles in a week;
roustabouts most nights, initiation rites – streaking through
the floodlit truck-park, thirty-odd below, in bunny boots
and hard-hat, bollocks greased; rooming with an ex-con
dope fiend out of Bald Knob, Arkansas; guys stir-crazy
for their R&R while you stayed cool with yoga, meditation,
wiring off each pay-check to your new account back home.
And so the months edged by; the pipe, the pump-stations
took shape; you dreaming night and day of moving south,

Tulik to Valdez, Hull to Hampshire, the haulage fleet
you'd build again, how you'd wipe that courtroom smile
clean off her face. And so, and soon, it came to pass:
the cottage in the Forest, latest Lotus, you driving out
one crisp and star-filled night beside your new love,
not drunk, not speeding, maybe high on happiness –
the patch of ice or oil you hit, and skidded from
toward the trees, no bigger than a dime, a nickel set against
the white and glistening danger you'd escaped unharmed,
the billion barrels loaded since along Prince William Sound.

Daily Mail

25ml Rye
25ml Amer Picon
25ml Orange Squash
3ds Orange Bitters

Shake & strain

It's daybreak, I tug at the curtain
and there's this immaculate limo
(blacked-over windows,
half the length of the street)
sliding soundlessly by.

Rubbing my eyes, I look up
but no, there's no neon, no
Caesar's Palace, just the same
washed-out, workaday sky
and down by the fence

the sign still points to Earith
and Chatteris as old Harry
in slippers, paper tucked
under one arm, lifts the tail
of his coat, scratches his arse

and shuffles back up the path.
It's too fucking early. Time to
darken things up again. Stretch
out the yawn, slip back into bed.
I like to know when I'm dreaming.

Clap of Thunder

25ml Dry Gin
25ml Rye Whisky
25ml Brandy

Shake & strain

A
long
haul it
was and
rain all the
way, though
nothing amiss
till somewhere
past Crewe, till
that ten-minute
pit-stop where
someone made
off with the CDs
cassettes,
left us silent and
tense and back in
the crawler-lane,
blinded by spray,
in fear of our lives,
despairing of any
way out, something
different, but that's
what you were –
smearing out of the

deluge, drenched in
that lay-by, grasping a
sign which no one
could read, that once you
climbed in we discovered
said Blackburn, though
we never made Man-
chester, not once you
pulled out the knife,
relieved us of
watches and cards
and near fifty in cash,
hopping out with that
grin, with two raps
on the roof, saying
lighten up girls
you'll still make the
funeral, then off
up the slope with
your sidekick, the rain.

Amsterdam

37ml Gin
12ml Triple Sec
18ml Mandarin Juice

Shake with a glassful of broken ice
& pour unstrained

"You? A cop?" Even then, your sister just laughed
but she spoke for us all, Mr Laid-Back-and-Languid
Mr Spliff-Hazy-Hippy, as you came round in bed
with your head shaved and bandaged,
as your scattergun words were a throwback to Java
as you pointed at water and called it a pillow
raged at the nurses
while memory returned in small pieces –
that motorbike spinning away
as you shuffled through Rehab then back to a flat
you said wasn't yours, where you tidied obsessively
threw out the leathers, your Hendrix, stopped smoking reefers
knocked off the booze,
began mouthing doctrinaire views,
enrolled in cadet-school
toughed out the whispers of *rijstpikhaak-monkey*
made it with honours from the Academy –
wound up patrolling your very own neighbourhood,
fastidious with paperwork,
booking muggers and dealers, those you once scored from,
soon with the vice-squad
some of it heavy, much of it crazy –
like the punter whose playtime went painfully wrong
you carting him off still attached to the Hoover-pipe –
back to that place where you'd railed at the doctors
where the past was all scrambled, your future unravelled
and the rest of us laughed
at the very idea.

Tornado

50ml Silver Tequila
25ml White Créme de Cacao
25ml Double Cream

Shake & strain
Sprinkle with grated chocolate

When ink dries and the words spin off, what havoc

will ensue – your scent, your sashay trailed across the page
as pure pheremone, setting men and dogs trembling?

Even here to reveal you – your skin a dark river,
the rise of your blouse like wild orchids, *Les Deux Pitons*

outlined at dusk at Soufrière – even clothed
your legs, your behind induce moaning, delirium.

Someone distracted this instant, already falling in love,
just missed his connection, flight-call, intended bride;

debates are swayed by a Senator's rapture, A-graders flounder,
artists abandon their portraits assailed by inexplicable visions

even women, unhinged with envy, turn feral
walk out for good, become someone other –

look, it's happening right here, right ahead, as we stride
hand-in-hand into town, a bus flashes past, jumps a red

there's squealing of rubber, horn squawks and sirens –
don't blame the poor guy, he just glimpsed you, you're caught

on his retina, he's a long way from here, full of darker
more tantalising colour as your fingers tighten

round mine and even through our gloves, electricity.

"Call me **what you like,** only **give me** some **vodka.**"

Russian Proverb

AWOL

12ml Amaretto
25ml Scotch
12ml Dry Orange Curacao
18ml Lime Juice

Shake & strain into a glass filled with broken ice
Garnish with an orange wedge

So what is it with writers and liquor?
With the crafted lines and messed-up minds,
the blurring of crazy and sane,
rapture, despair in the same pair of hands?

Look at the poets. Chatterton, Beddoes, Berryman, Kees.
Jarrell or Thomas, Sexton and Crane ...

Take any one. Take Crane.
                            Knocking back
jug after jug – bootleg gin, bad applejack –
out on the lam with a young Laura Riding,
strung out, hazy by morning
staring out from his desk on Columbia Heights
fighting for language
bold as his now-mythic Bridge

greying at thirty – swollen and blotched –
friends, mirrors, advice – everything shunned,
typewriter hurled to the night, to rattle
its keys on the frozen ground

while he wove through Montmartre
spouting *Tamburlaine* – throttle wide open,
each scene a blast –

back in Brooklyn would prowl
along Sands Street, milking each sailor-bar
for some jaded *encore*
(shark's-tooth there at his neck
on its tightening noose)

would plead and weep for their loyalty,
then rage at betrayal.

They knew – how they knew –
these late-night litanies,
these juice-soaked refrains:

Listen, you fools –
I am Baudelaire
Whitman
Marlowe
Christ …

but never, not even once, was he
Harold Hart Crane.

Starboard Light

30ml Sloe Gin
15ml Crème de Menthe
15ml Lemon Juice

Shake & strain

They fished him from the sea at night, a distance
from Land's End. Assumed him just another

sucked out willingly or terrified from shore –
maybe pushed or fallen overboard – certain, anyway

to have a name once science and procedure
got to work. Pathology. The trawl for dental charts

and fingerprints. So details circulated, seasons
passed but still he lay there, chilled and tagged

until the final inquest: *Deceased White Male*, 5'10",
11 stone, no papers, jewellery, just one befitting scar –

a horizontal question-mark that stretched
from forehead to right ear – *particularly prominent*

the coroner declared, *because of his receding hair.*
The saddest thing's that anyone should die

and not be missed. Recording then an open verdict,
releasing *whoever he might be* for unmarked burial

in a Penzance churchyard, overlooking open sea.

Zipper

37ml Cachaça or White Rum
37ml Kahlua
25ml Double Cream
1 teaspoon Baileys

Shake & strain into a glass
Sprinkle with grated chocolate

If he'd kept it shut
        his trousers up
his pants in place
        his brain engaged

known when to stop
        not touched a drop
and spent less time
        so well reclined

if he'd thought of others
        loved his mother
didn't scram
        when shit hit fan

had stayed at home
        paid back each loan
knew how to cry
        and never lied

he would have been
        a duller man
we wouldn't miss
        his recklessness

   his easy-come and easy-go.
      And though
   he caused a load of grief
      he was at least

   true to himself, his gods.
      What's lost
   isn't what he might've been –
      just what he was.

Bull Dog

Drop ice into a tumbler, then add

50ml Dry Gin
25ml Lemon Juice
1 small spoonful Sugar Syrup or Gomme
Fill up with chilled Ginger Ale

Stir & serve

If I see you look at her that way again
If you don't piss off back into the soddin' rain
If you're not gone before what's in this glass
If you want to see your whole life flashing past
If you think you'll pull a bird with hair like that
If you're telling me she'd fancy such a twat
If your Dad had only hung on to his clothes
If you're wanting five ringed knuckles up y'nose
If the eyes round here weren't all so bleedin' lost
If one sick fuck among us gave a toss
If your job or the barman's was for us
If you try to say it's you who needs a chance
If you want to be the one without a voice
If you've half a brain it's time you made a choice
If I were you I'd move and change your name
If I ever see you look at her
If you ever cross my fucking path again.

Great Secret

75ml Dry Gin
6ml Lillet
1ds Angostura

Shake & strain

Half the world was there too – anarchists, hippies,
Hell's Angels – like they'd come straight from Woodstock.
And with that kind of line-up (Donovan, Baez, The Who
Cohen, The Doors, Moody Blues) even then
you could sense it was history. The site was just vast,
more like a small city

we were part of the village backstage, this army
of caravans, tents and marquees serving fry-ups and
flagons of tea, keeping the roadies, gofers and crewmen
happy, crashing out from each marathon shift
for a few hours of kip, catching drifts of the music,
glimpses of Morrison (sex on a stick)

serving Joni an omelette (the miserable cow)
but mostly too busy or knackered to venture out front.
What's more, and though this was August, it turned
muddy and wet. By the final night, Sunday,
the cold I had had since arrival was bad –
I felt sick, wanted out –

when this voice at the counter says, *Hold it,*
I'll give you a fiver for that. I look up,
see this ponytailed guy as he holds out the money.
He's eyeing the small folded wrapper, the cold-cure
I've pulled from my shirt. *Have a heart*, the guy says
Jimi's on soon

and he's run a bit short. Before I can think, never mind
tip the stuff in hot water, the note's in my palm and
the guy and the wrapper are gone. Still, five bloody quid
was ok! Minutes after, I saw him again, one of the gang
leading Hendrix onstage. Heard the roar, Jimi's intro
of *God Save The Queen*,

Sgt. Pepper. Not many days later, of course, news broke
he was dead: OD'd while asleep, 'choked on his vomit' –
that was the verdict. Pipecleaner-thin, we all knew
his habit. Even so, I felt strange at the time, went quiet
when the subject came up. And thirty years on,
even now

when I hear *Purple Haze* or *Watchtower* blare out, I still
sometimes wonder. Picture those final few hours in his
girlfriend's apartment, bombed out already, desperate for
something to shoot, pop or snort. Fumbling through pockets,
coming up with my small crumpled wrapper, that same
Beechams Powder ...

Novocaine

37ml Pisang Ambong
18ml Gin
6ml Green Charteuse
50ml Sparkling Bitter Lemon

Shake with half a glassful of
broken ice and pour unstrained
Add the lemon

The long chair reclines and the needle goes in, into
the gum, under the skin. Another extraction, another
reminder that nothing holds fast, or not for much longer.

The best they can do by way of distraction
is fixed to the ceiling: an aerial view
of the streets of my town. Lying there tense

as he's fixing the clamps, I locate the car-park,
back out of there pronto, make a beeline for home.
Am soon eating lunch, set up with a Scotch –

a full set of teeth and a mouth free of fillings.
Missing you, I sit back, begin dreaming
of Novocaine – all those other bright dawns,

false prophets, saviours and gods. All of them
promised, set our fragile hearts racing, then dummied
our brains. Amphetamine, barbies, a few drops of acid;

one pop of E and a smidgen of H. A quick toke
of ganja, a pure line of China, this hot little pill …
Right, we're all done, sir. Rinse out if you will.

Again I head home: blood on the tongue, ache in the jaw.
No more impostors, OK? Let's trust in endorphins,
adrenaline, the rush of each other. Love's natural law.

Green Room

20ml Brandy
40ml French Vermouth
2ds Curacao

Shake & strain

Still here, in the thicket of hair,
the forty-year groove in the bone
of the boy who was maybe two inches
from not coming home –

tearing outside in a clatter of studs,
making straight for the short-cut
(as the smallest ones did)
through the four steel struts

and square of dark space
that propped up the Green Room.
And as his ears rung, as the nausea came
and his team-mates spun

as his knees dissolved in the crisp afternoon,
as something smooth and warm
slithered over his skull and on
down his neck and he finally went down

most thought he was acting –
hamming it up in the chorus-line turn
that only last night
he had practised above them

still the clown, still oblivious
of anguish or challenge or keeping his head down.
One day from having to duck, not ducking
enough. Even now, I reach up and touch him.

Scotch Mist

Shake 50ml Scotch with crushed ice
Pour unstrained
Add twist of lemon
Serve with short straws

Bound for Inverness
the cloud comes down off Craigellachie.
Beams full on, we creep along at twenty –
no sign of tail-lights, other cars. She peers from map
to screen, says it doesn't look that far, and then:

You ever play Scotch Mist? You know, describing Zero –
as many ways you can?

        I glance across, the edge
        clear in her tone, but shake my head. *Sure, why not.*
        Give anything a go. About the only thing we haven't tried.
        So she starts, I drive.

Zero, zip, zilch, nothing,
 nil, nought, nobody, no-one, no,
  not one, not a thing, not a bit, nonesuch,
   never, not at all, not anywhere, nowhere,
    chimera, utopia, emptiness, fantasy, fancy, a cipher,
     mirage, hallucinate, metaphor, semblance, resemblance, non-
      existence, non-being, nonentity, nullity, nonsense, absence,
       non-appearance, non-attendance, a void, a gap, a lack, lacuna,
        omission, illusion, excision, extinction, oblivion ... forgotten.

We're edging along. Just moving forward.
    Alone in the fog, in the echoing car.

        Something looms up and is gone:
           a signpost for Aviemore.

           Nice game, I tell her, keeping my eyes on the road.
           So why does it feel like I drew the short straw?

" The **bar** was our **altar**. "

Caitlin Thomas

Brainstorm

50ml Irish Whisky
2ds Benedictine
2ds French Vermouth

Shake & strain

Ah, Dylan. D.T. With initials like that
you had a head start, soon made it clear
that your fast route from Swansea
would be well-fuelled with beer.

And then you met Caitlin – where else
but a bar? – drew up your joint mantra:
Moderation kills. Do all to excess.
And each bar was your altar.

Between the 3rd and 8th pint you were
magical, witty: half-genius, half-clown.
Why's it mad to write poetry but sane that we
all lunch at one? To me it's the other way round.

The trail led to Soho (The Wheatsheaf, The Horseshoe)
propped in the corners on a soggy, slow-burn;
thence to New York (The Chelsea, Algonquin)
bow-tie askew, drink's little propeller beginning to turn.

Pop-eyed, heavy-lipped, baggy-brown-suited,
led to each lectern then making them gasp
with the power, the control, that baritone rumble,
all that emerged through the thick piggy mask.

Whatever night you went into, you never went gently.
Eighteen straight whiskies – for sure that's the record!
As your Cattleanchor said: *we had to wallow in shit*
to soar to the peaks. Peaks you know well, under Milk Wood.

Garryowen

50ml Jamieson
25ml Galliano
25ml Rose's Lime & Lemon
ds Egg White
ds Crème de Banane
ds Orange Squash

Shake & strain

The Yorkshire Moors. November. Raw. Hooped
in red and black, we steam from the pavilion, fifteen
local heroes wreathed in embrocation, whooped
on to the field with whistles, catcalls, stamping feet.
The touchlines heave with teachers, parents, mates –
plus two full coach-loads up from Leeds. Today it's Us
and Them; the Toffs against the Grammar; the Papists
v. the Prods. Our end-of-season showdown, no love lost.
They (shaven-headed, big as bouncers, backstreet bruisers)
lounge and snigger while we stretch. Beside them, it's a fact,
we look like lightweights, kids v. men, a bunch of losers
but from the off were into them like terriers, our pack's
there first to every ball, recycling to the backs who scissor
in the centre, spin wide to the wings, launch towering kicks
that drop with ice on. Long before the break they're
five tries down, open-mouthed and steaming, thirty points adrift.
The half-time talk's redundant, we've got them by the throat:
drop goals, force penalties at leisure, try out all our riffs –
it's almost too predictable when, just off the pitch, their coach
is spotted racing past the line-out, squaring up to Fr. Abbot,
half-a-dozen monks, maniacal in wind-blown black,
who've hopped and flapped like rooks throughout, like zealots
crazed with self-belief: *Go on! – BH ... BH! Great stuff! Crackerjack!*

or *CF, boys! ... CF!* – diplomatic shorthand that's finally provoked
a claim of cheating, coaching, calling codes. It's mayhem
as the whistle blows, we all pile in, and now the bloke's
accusing them of language unbecoming of a priest. Translation
hasn't seemed to help – to know their cries were only *Bury Him!*
and *Catholic Fury!* But maybe he was wondering, as we did,
if these wayward mascots – these worldly men of God –
if their presence, prayers or wild-eyed invocations are the reason
why, for three whole seasons now, we're still unbeaten.

Alexei's Sister

25ml Dry Gin
25ml Crème de Menthe
25ml Fresh Cream

Shake & strain
in a Martini glass

Until she said it

no one in years
had called him
'romantic'.

He hadn't
brought her flowers

whisked her away
for a weekend
in Paris

or fallen to his knees
with a ring.

All he'd done
was tell her he loved her;
what a strong and beautiful
woman
she was.

Even now she just smiles
or laughs down the phone
with embarrassment –

as though she's been given
the earth.

But she, of course, is the gift.

For proving, with love
it's never the end of the line;
for awaking this much-missed
companion – here again, now,
beating hard in his chest.

Just like she said,
the Old Romantic
is back.

Dunlop

20ml Sherry
40ml Rum
1ds Angostura

Shake & strain

Last green, last chance as you stroll to the pin
in the reddening light and I pace out eight strides –
slowing it down, fired by your confident grin.

Crouched down the bank, each blade becomes clear.
One longer stem. That studmark dead on the line.
Somewhere deep, taking shape, it's already here –

the ball's roll and bend, the gentle compression
flowing up through the hands as it topspins away
from the glint of smooth metal –

vividly white as I settle and picture it, climbing the rise
then taking the break, a tracing of light in the gathering
dark – its path slow enough for your premature smile

as you tug out the stick then stand there alarmed
in the last of the sun with the hawk overhead,
the egg-yolks of gorse, faint hum of cars

with each bead of sweat and the heat in my grip,
the almondy scent and ten shades of green
as it reaches and hangs there, then drops from the lip.

A Fine Balance

25ml Vodka
12ml Gin
12ml Crème de Cassis
ds Lime Juice

Add equal parts
Bitter Lemon & Tonic Water

Sure, we all have our secrets.
How else to get by?

Honesty – can you imagine?
I can. I know. That way

believe me, is danger and pain.
Here, let me prove it.

Right now you can sit there,
everything's fine.

That's because we have secrets.
But if I told you mine –

like, say, I'd not touched
a drink in six months.

That I once couldn't stop.
That I'm now with AA.

That my stepfather screwed me,
six to sixteen – once, twice a day.

That I never feel clean.
That I'm here on a test –

two nights a week
to prove I've the strength.

And tonight I feel
right on the edge

really drawn to that taste –
even nursing the dregs

of this last bitter lemon.
See? Now I've no secrets.

And now plenty bothers you.
Now you are itching to go.

Pete

15ml French Vermouth
15ml Italian Vermouth
30ml Gin
2ds Maraschino
Small spoonful of Orange Juice

Shake & strain

We'd fooled them, turned the odds on their head –
pushing out of the final exam, that's how it felt

two-thousand days, now those sacrosanct hours
of madness and mayhem were ours –

that long moonless night like a blessing,
taking us under its wing

as we stole up the clocktower, hoisted the effigy,
dismantled the gamesmaster's Mini

reassembled it inside the chapel,
strung tampons from rafters like miniature candles

3am, made that final planned charge down the valley –
past classrooms, goalposts, throwing off clothes all the way –

scaling the fence to the pool,
you ahead, rushing straight for the springboard, kicking off shoes –

twenty years on I can see it, that treacherous glisten
as I'm jolted awake, still lost for a reason

as you call back *we made it!*
as I catch the pale flash of your feet

why they drained out the water that same afternoon,
our last day of school.

Southern Belle

25ml Bourbon
12ml Southern Comfort
12ml white Crème de Cacao
1 teaspoon green Crème de Menthe
25ml Peach Juice
25ml Whipping Cream

Shake & strain

Palmettos, bougainvillea
Spanish moss cobwebs adrift in the live oaks
and everywhere history –
Daughters of the Revolution, Civil War cannon
still trained on Fort Sumpter

fresh into town they'd found him a guide
just as memorable, quirky –
flame-haired in a gossamer dress
smother and glare forming dew on her skin

till after an hour
she led him out of that hothouse
and into the o welcome chill
of a condo-block close to the harbour

just droppin bah
in that languid, Old-Money drawl
as they rose in the small service lift
to a five-million view of the ocean
a chrome-and-glass pad like a showhome
just a caretaking job, she explained
watering plants, checking mail

showing round possible buyers
while friends were in Europe

you know – 'interested parties', she said
catching his eye
in a way they both recognised

that with no further thought
led to clothes on the floor
to an art-nouveau rug and grand double-bed
to the heart-stopping chime of the bell
as she came on his tongue
(little yelps stifled in terror)

then the one-minute scramble to dress,
to conceal all the evidence

her opening the door – the couple who stood there
a full day ahead of their prearranged viewing –

waving them in with bravura
with that flush at her neck, self-satisfied smile

to rooms reeking of heat now, of musk and risk,
another kind of trade.

Sanctuary

12ml Cointreau
12ml Amer Picon
25ml Dubonnet

Shake & strain

Kerry throws back the dregs, lights up another, says
Look, I'm ok, what the hell, good riddance anyway
and we nod, like a coven around her
trying hard to remember how many she's had now –
Sal's fiddling and folding a dead bag of crisps,
she goes back to chewing her nails –

shit, I'm strung out, Kerry coughs, *haven't slept
since the dumb bastard left*
smoke's a fog round her face, like she's
fading away, least she had him to lose
I am thinking, but how sad is that
come on, get a grip –

almost three years, three painless years
without screaming and fists, that stale stink of drink
and half-hearted pawing – you just got your life back
don't blow it, don't blow it
LAST ORDERS NOW, LAST ORDERS PLEASE
mine's a vodka and orange, says Kerry

Liz gets the round in, Donna trips to the Ladies
Sal needs the chippie, laughs Jane, *if she's chews any more
she'll be down to the elbow.* And it comes back again
how it felt going in, that manslaughter knife, into bone, into flesh
through the arms that he raised … *Cheers then*, says Kerry.
What is it with men? Such a fight, such a long bloody fight.

"A **soft drink** turneth away **company**."

Oliver Herford

Babies

40ml Apricot Brandy
20ml Fresh Cream
ds Dry Gin

Shake & strain

Me, I never had children, he says, nodding at mine
as I ease in beside him, hunched on his barstool.
The door to the garden stands open: they're shrieking
with joy, playing Tag round the trees, while here
punters lean to the counter, jaws set, grasping fivers
and tenners, daring the girl not to turn to them next.
Pretty wee things. He draws on a roll-up. Music swims
from the jukebox. *And a fine handsome woman.* Barely catch
what he says, read his lips asking *Twins?* – take a deep
inward breath though of course, like the rest, he is curious
and in truth we are used to this now. *Yes*, I say
Bo and Mai. Cambodian. Orphans. Been nearly eight years ...

Alone, overstretched, the barmaid is close to defeat – you can
see it – the cream on a Caffrey's spills over a glass, someone
tells her to lick it, others laugh. He just stares at the optics.
Will you look at them there, lined up like the newborn
and shiny with promise – each with its own little teat.
Warming the heart, eh? Source of our worry and grief.
London Silk, Commissar, Smirnoff – I follow the point
of his cigarette – *Courvoisier, Bells, Southern Comfort ...*
A tilt of the head and I'm fixed in his wet rheumy gaze.
*You'll indulge an old fool? These are **my** babies. Won't you*
name me your pleasure, if ever the fair maid comes by?

Sunset

17ml Light Honey
35ml Lemon Juice
70ml Golden Tequila

Mix & serve with shaved ice

(Mallory Square, Key West)

In matchstick silhouette
the Creole mute performs
his nightly trick against
this world-end sunset:

steps in and folds himself
like rubber into one no-
bigger- than- a- toolbox
almost- foursquare prop.

Unexercised spectators,
we creak with nervous
laughter in our frames –
our skeletons all ratchets

brackets, cogs unbending
in each fractious part, each
knuckle-crack and clicking
disc. So it goes: contortion

and survival moulded into
art. This box, now closing,
that we edge toward, away
from, chalk-marked *RISK*.

Henry's Last Hurrah

37ml Sweet Sherry
12ml Scotch
12ml Dry Sherry
12ml Dry Vermouth
1 teaspoon Drambuie
6ml Lemon Juice
87ml Lemonade

Add to an ice-filled glass
with a half-slice of lemon

Myopic, acned 'Blears' – nicknames, doubles
from the start – cack-handed, studious,
ambushed by the jocks between the icehouse
and the railroad, arms pinned, raw bones
wriggling free, dashing
for the tracks, the first of many
yearnings

pacing the quad at Clare, wringing your hands –
overcome with hysterical laughter
at the critics mystified:
Long may they rave! Sing them
a lullaby, then hit them
over the head!

sailing home, disembarking
from the *Îsle de France* transformed
in beard and tweeds, a DH Lawrence lookalike
more English than the English,
a new & tewwible Bewwyman the Campbells called you –
brilliant, witty, fun, repelling, selfish ...
more than a bit ridiculous

dismissing Dr Shea, the therapy, and turning
to your dreams, trawling up
the Songs – *that Pierrot's universe, that glory
of the age* – running drafts by Cal, buttonholing
barmen, shoeshine boys, calling Tate at 3am
*Listen pal, you must hear this!
Delicious, truly!* –

groomed affected youth
transmuting into Henry, Mr Heartbreak, Pussycat
Sir Bones – the shaggy, shambling
crack-up on the juice

chasing fame but finding it
another crown of thorns – laid up in the ward,

foot mangled by a car as you alighted, rolling –
competing for attention even then,
Kate & newborn just along the hall

yet through the drunks
a teacher conscientious to a fault –
taxied trembling from the clinic to your class
blue eyes rheumy (*peanut-faced beneath a Homburg*
noted Bellow) turning numbered prep cards, shaky-voiced
then back, sweating, to the cab –
back to contemplate

Step One
your Kate & little Twiss
Recovery
Delusions
pitchers of Martini
Addresses to the Lord
your circle small and closing

Mother bleating on
Daddy in the yard, face shot away
that icehouse and the moaning of the train
your mirror-image ancient,
glistening, grey –

edging down the steps
and into New Year sleet, the morning shuttle out
toward the campus, alighting
with the crowd but passing by
the glassed-in walkway, shuffling on in bitter cold along the bridge,
almost making it
before the huge half-frozen river beckoned you –
to clamber to the waist-high beam,
to balance there, stare down
to shrouded bank and coal-dock, naked trees,
oblivious to others halting, powerless –
taking in a final flailing gesture
as you tilted out, let
                    go.

Smokey

20ml Bourbon Whiskey
20ml Marie Brizard Apricot
20ml Sweet Martini
2ds Lemon Juice

Shake & strain

In from the garden, still later from the bath
it clung on – in your hair, in my sweater's
thick weave – the last bonfire won't let us
forget these years, not the black ring of grass
scorched there outside, the heat on our skin,
snap and spit of mildewed boxes, or wet leaves
spinning their ash-ghosts: what we breathed
in building the fire, nor through its burning.
Is it why I'm down early today, breaking habit,
mist on the lawn, house silent, lighting up
this first cigarette since Frèjus, thirty-odd
years ago? Tapped from a long-buried packet
of *Gitanes*, cellophane-fresh, faint still
with pine-scent, now it glows in the gloom
like a tender's fog-light and I see you again
through the same bluish haze, pausing to lean
on the rake, hand raised, brushing hair from your eyes
as if on a steam-shrouded platform, waving goodbye.

S.W.1

25ml Vodka
25ml Campari
25ml Orange Juice
10ml Egg White

Shake & strain

The room overlooks Piccadilly.

All week it waits, breathing alone, waiting for Wednesday,
the scratch of a key in the lock.
He'll arrive first, bearing roses and wine, hot
from the courts, breathless from climbing four flights.
Fetch glasses, replenish the vase, fill the bucket with ice.
But today,
the week the clocks change,
he stares long and hard in the mirror,
raises the heavy sash window,
falls back on the still-pristine bed
and empties his head
of the clamour below as the lace-curtains billow.
She's already with him: the burn of her flesh,
the moment both he and the room, all of London falls silent,
holding its breath,
awaiting her cry.

What can he tell her? When will he dare? How will he lie?

Slipstream

12ml Brandy
12ml Grand Marnier
12ml Lillet
12ml Orange-Passion Fruit
2ds Angostura
10ml Egg White

Shake & strain

Back then, we had to force ourselves
to look. Beneath the stone, the bed.
Along the shelf behind the books.

Then gradually confronted what we
feared. Grew nonchalant with grubs
and dark and dust – until the next

(or was it same?) unfaceable arrived.
And so today it stole up yet again:
tugging at our furtive, rear-view mirror

glance. That pelt and broken back –
still riffling in our slipstream as we
whistled by. Far worse, the glassy eye

which wouldn't leave our own,
which followed us along the broken line
where luck leapt out to dazzle it last night.

Wobbly Knee

25ml Amaretto di Sarano
25ml Kahlua
12ml Vodka
18ml Coconut Cream
25ml Double Cream

Blend briefly in a glassful
of crushed ice
Sprinkle with grated chocolate

Legacy, by sixty, of the glory years – your reign as Gloucester's
squash and tennis king: crumbling cartilage, dodgy joints,
hips and knees that took you out onto the links, but then
would tremble in the mildest breeze, sabotage that once-robotic swing.

But forget the game: at well past fifty you still wiped the floor
with me. Hard now to believe. Or how – for father, son,
inarticulate in love – these were trials of strength
we had to win, that mattered to us both – and far too much.

You weren't the greatest golfer nor the perfect Dad
and if one learns by imitation then I learnt the faults as well.
Sometimes even hated you for dragging me along,
weekend after weekend, into biting winds and rain-swept dunes.

But I thank you now. For suffering those brattish tantrums
as a ball banana-ed out-of-bounds, plugged deep beneath
some Himalayan bunker face or horseshoed round the hole.
I shudder at that anger: how I'd slam the flagstick in the cup,

snap a putter on my knee, hurl an iron disgustedly away –
whistling past you into deepest rough. For if today I'm not
that same obnoxious kid, that same damn fool, have calmed
and grown a little, won some county caps, got the handicap to 2 –

the good, as much, is down to you. And if a single memory remains
to prove amid those strange and serious days we also laughed,
it's this. You – about to play, settling in your stance.
The three of us – partner and opponents – quiet,

a few steps off and watching as, beneath the folds
of winter clothes, the astrakhan with ear-flaps down,
the burning beacon of your nose, you make that last
adjusting movement – a final tiny flexing in the knees –

a bird, we'd think, about to settle on its nest –
before, too swift to register, you whip the club away
and chop down in a blur as if to stun or kill
some helpless, wounded thing ... then swivel round

and face us, scowling – mystified yet furious at our lapse
in etiquette – *Well, where is it? What's so bloody funny?
Come on, did you see it?* – but by now we're rolling
uncontrollably like upturned beetles on the frosted ground –

aching, speechless, disbelieving what we've seen as you
exclaim and fix us with a look that only makes us
howl the more – aware we'll never see the like again.
How, driven hard and straight into the frozen turf

the ball had lifted off not forward but in a perfect
upward arc and then, as you ducked round toward
the target, dropped and vanished with the timing
of a conjurer into the pocket of your windproof jacket.

Cowboy

40ml Rye Whisky
20ml Cream

Shake & strain

Uncle Harry would simply appear –
walk in the back-door clutching flowers and a bottle –
turn to Mum, think better of it, then to Rosie and me, arms wide
and we'd run there, get spun through the air before she could
smother our joy.

It wasn't till later, much later, I found that he had little choice
if he wanted to see us – she wouldn't invite him, this reprobate
dangerous brother – who refused to fall in, bow down, tidy up,
who preferred to keep moving, everyone guessing.
Only one thing we knew: he always brought a Zane Grey

and after dinner's faint murmur – sudden gunshots of laughter
up through the floorboards – he'd come creaking upstairs like a cowpoke
in heavy spurred boots, nearly crack our small beds in saying goodnight
and tell us, as if he'd just left there, of Tombstone, Dodge City,
of gold-panners, lynch-mobs, rustlers and outlaws – till we fell fast asleep.

We loved the voices he'd do, his slow honest sheriff,
slippery cardsharp, henpecking wife – though Mum looked disgusted
(like she'd sucked on a lemon) if ever I told her.

Tuh, just a load of hot air, the big lummox.
Stand him in front of these clothes, he'd dry them in no time!
But you know they're just stories, Sam –

don't let him frighten you. She couldn't concede
we could love this great force –
blown in like a blast of hot dust, spilling cups

and routine, turning things on their heads.
Or simply lifting us onto his knee – an oak-solid bench
outside some saloon – whispering *best you say nothing, hey podnas?*
Not with this price on my head. Guess I'll saddle up now, then wait
until sundown. Hole up in them mountains a while, due west of town.

Thistle

50ml Scotch Whisky
25ml Italian Vermouth
2ds Angostura

Shake & strain

Walk into a bar. Any bar.
        What are you looking for?

Companionship?
        Solitude?
Oblivion?
        Escape?
A glance?
        A score?
A listener?
        A talker?
A lover?
        A looker?
Sophocles?
        Chaucer?
Bukowksi?
        A hooker?
A pint before home?
        A last drink alone?

On the rocks,
you say.
Best make it a double

and the bartender pauses,
catches your eye,

understands you have ordered it
all.

Deep Sea

35ml French Vermouth
35ml Dry Gin
ds Pernod
ds Orange Bitters

Shake & strain

We float out on a sea of silence, masked
from one another, weightless, barely human –
signalling our language now. Swimming on,
the warmth, the coral drops away like vertigo,
the ice-cold ocean's swift as grey half-shadow
scattering the blue tang, gar and surgeon-fish –
sure where we are not, safe where we are not,
twisting from us bubbles of anxiety as it
hurtles by along the ledge, down into the dark.

Ward Eight

50ml Rye
12ml Orange Juice
12ml Lemon Juice
teaspoon Grenadine

Shake & strain

For panic, rage, self-pity, shock
(an absent wife)
take four days on the ward
with manic Phoebus

                    currently so high
                    he's tripping on fresh air and dreams

and let him teach you
rudimentary twelve-bar blues
on Tracy, his electric bass.

                    Backlit, haloed –
                    plectrum glinting like a hypnotist's –
                    revelations splinter
                    faster than his tongue can lead

yeah Tracy and her tracer-bullets zing!
the Gulf the oil that's mir – connect?
myrhh the gift of God whose frankincense is
innocence and gold gold leaf ...

                    until your own despair and grief's
                    dissolving with each strum, each
                    painful chord your bitten fingers play

So why you cryin' man?
you got real style …

                    because the demons for a while
                    are stilled, your breathing eased.
                    Even the nurse across the ward,
                    that half-familiar profile, raven hair
                    you now can face, smile weakly back to
                    as she leaves.

Ceasefire

25ml Scotch
25ml Cherry Brandy
25ml Dry Vermouth
75ml Lemonade

Add to an ice-filled glass
Garnish with a lemon slice and a cherry

Forget victory.

Forget how
that deafening clash

turned to
wrestling of wills

battles bloody
and many

skirmishes, sieges
years of

attrition. Forget
how neither retreated

firing off salvos
scourging with words

with intimate
knowledge

and how to deploy it.
Hold on

to what shone
like a blade

to what smoulders
like pitch

that terrible beauty
its still-fading echo:

I love you.

"The **hardest thing** about being a **bartender** is figuring out who is **drunk** and who is just **stupid**."

Richard Braunstein

Firebird

37ml Silver Tequila
12ml Crème de Banane
12ml Lime Juice
50ml Lemonade

Add to a glass three-quarters
filled with crushed ice

Sure, Carl was a poser. Modelled on Cruise, he thought himself
smoother. Darker and harder. A million times cooler.

Most days you'd laugh, others you envy these guys –
the attention, the women, the easy applause –

and sometimes (admit it) we're longing for life
to spin round and deck them, lay them out senseless.

Still, what happened to him you'd not even wish
on the ultimate prick. And whatever he was, Carl wasn't that.

* * *

We worked at *The Catacomb* then. Best bar in town,
the one place to be. Down a flight from the street

to this cavernous vault: arches, low ceilings, soft candle glow.
Hint of red plush and Dave Brubeck, alcoves in shadow.

Come weekends, place really heaving, there'd be five or six of us
working full tilt. Shrine to the grape and the grain

and where people came for the ultimate cocktail – Carl's beat
and mine. Ok, none worked the speedrail like him –

he was the showman, the joker, your real barman juggler
going non-stop, blessed with the patter ... where I am

the bookworm, the scholar by nature – precise with
each mixture and measure – less flashy, less fast.

But the punters need both. Entertainers, informers.
Laughter and history. A sense of pride in the art.

* * *

That night, as ever, he had his routine. Took the first break
as we reached 'beer o'clock'; moved round the bar,

sank a couple of brandies, his stiffening shot. As word
got around the first cries would go up, the clapping would start –

Bring on the Fireman! Go for it, Carl! – and slowly they'd form
this aisle in the crowd. Even then he'd play them a while, hang back

as if knackered, wave them away, wait till he had them all baying
then hold up his hands, give a shrug, say 'OK', and we'd dim

the spots further as I passed him his baton – Galliano, that long
slim bottle plugged at the neck with a rag-flame of lighter-fuel –

and off he would go, spinning streamers of light through
the phalanx of cheering – twirling and weaving – for a minute or so

even we would be gasping. And it all went to plan, that particular night,
till his showpiece finale – till he held the struck match to his lips

and blew them a blast of that 100-proof brandy, a fire-eater's kiss,
as up on the street, at the very same second, someone opened a door ...

Next thing we knew, Carl was a torch. Flailing his arms, down
on the floor, rolling and thrashing. The whole place was screaming.

Someone grabbed at a siphon and sprayed him, half-missed.
Two of us hurdled the bar, smothered the flames with our jackets.

* * *

They kept him for months on one ward or another. Most of the damage
was down in his throat, deep in the lungs. There were grafts

to his hands, to his lips, cheeks and chin. His eyes were ok,
though much of his hair was burnt off or singed. By the time

they discharged him they said he was lucky – at his age the skin
was still supple. *Give it time, mind the sunlight, it may still recover.*

And he took this to heart. Said he'd find a way back, any route
save for ending up scarred. So he bought in a three-month supply –

food and books, an exercise bike – all that he'd need – then blacked-out
the windows, painted the walls just as dark, and for ten-to-twelve weeks

never stirred from the house. And it worked. When at last Carl emerged
people looked at his face in amazement – not a blemish or flaw, no sign

of trauma. Some said he looked younger, 'reborn', a new man –
and in truth, to the casual eye, you might think he was cured.

But remember, I knew him. And he works in a bank now.
Won't touch a drop. Has never been back to the bars.

Crossbow

20ml Gin
20ml Cointreau
20ml Crème de Cacao

Shake & strain

If you're looking for
sanity
self-expression
a way to kick back
at your parents
then take up karate
date only hustlers
make love in the street
base-jump or free-fall
right to the limit
hitchhike the Arctic
take vows and retreat
forget the career path
risk a calculus class
find the longest odds
and stake all you've got
pierce the machinery
flaunt biker tattoos
deal counterfeit tender
embrace that neurosis
confront every phobia
have death round for tea
take a crossbow to bed
and shoot out the TV
interrogate dust
chase the moon
with a sieve
but *please* –
show ultimate courage,
save us one cruelty:
don't write it down
and don't call it
poetry.

Upstairs

45ml Dubonnet
15ml Lemon Juice

Shake & strain

They left in a hurry was all
she would say, leading us round

this first place to feel like home
for a six-month let.

The back-bedroom
was small, lacked a bed –

it was hers, it went with her
she muttered, here in the doorway

though that suited you
with your own close at hand

plus a van-full of boxes.
You were glad of the dark extra space

of blue carpet, threw down
a sleeping-bag, cushions

amazed at all you packed in
to your very own Tardis –

its time-travel outlook
of back-to-back gardens,

that blowaway shed
for the Flymo, our bikes.

* * *

It's a month before he appears,
unannounced … *to check on the mail*

to glance at the transient names
on the shelf in the hall,

stay just long enough
to explain how they'd no heart to stay

(the three who were left)
in those days after finding her

curled like a child just asleep,
wrapped tight in the sheets.

She assumed it was flu – so did we –
but after she'd gone we simply felt

guilty, didn't know what to do
except scrub the place clean

get the bed to the tip, just pack up
and go. Mrs D thought it best

to say nothing, but I felt you should know.
Then, coffee untouched, he drove off

and that was the night you awoke –
sitting up sharp on the very same spot

feeling weird, you said later, *almost as if
I'd just spoken his name, that it hurt*

*just to think of him. Then I coughed,
the room grew familiar. I recalled who I was.*

Summer Rain

25ml Raspberry Purée
25ml Grapefruit Juice
25ml Pineapple Juice
50ml Orange Sherbet or Sorbet
25ml Lemonade

Blend briefly with half a glassful
of crushed ice
Add the lemonade
Garnish with seasonal fruit & straws

And as it fell –
raising hell against the roof,
dancing polkas on the patio –
we bolted to the summerhouse
rotating gently on its saucer-plinth
as if still searching for the sun –
and there among the swing-seat cushions,
cricket bats, your Dad's
abandoned telescope,
healed at last our long polarity –
your Arien directness,
my wary Scorpio –
till our rose-encircled planet spun so fast
the blooms were comets, quasars, red stars
flashing in our wake, our craft
a long way now from earth, that garden
under racing clouds,
a drying wind.

"They talk of my drinking, but never my thirst."

Scottish Proverb

Affinity

20ml French Vermouth
20ml Italian Vermouth
20ml Scotch Whisky
2ds Angostura
Slice of Lemon Peel

Shake & strain

Some moments are like that –
falling like gifts from another
dimension – Nostradamus, Copernicus, all the
snug-bar philosophers can never
explain them – all we can do is reach out
and hold on in gratitude –
to the raw clammy tongue of the fog,
that phosphorus glow as you led down a street
I knew couldn't exist – even the inn-sign,
The Wayward Apostle,
seemed prepared for our benefit –
falling into that comforting blast
of kinship and beer – *just a swift one*, you said –
though then, as things do, one led
to two, by when I was already blind
to your danger, pure spirit, caught
in the lock-in, that impromptu
all-nighter and all we still
cling to.

Beam Me Up Scotty

18ml Kahlua
18ml Crème de Banane
18ml Baileys

Make pousee-café
Serve in a shooter glass

And then it's done –

    last stragglers gone,
    bar and tables
    all wiped down,
    glasses polished
    hanging, stacked,
    rubbish bagged
    and out the back,
    ashtrays clean
    bar restocked
    cellar, storeroom
    checked and locked,
    the floors are swept
    the toilets mopped

before a final glance around –

    the CCTV tape's
    rewound (above the bar
    it winks its light,
    Greg waves *adiós*
    in black-and-white)
    the room goes dark,

we code and prime
the street-alarm
then part and head off
through the town
our collars up, our
shoulders hunched
(some to party, most
to kip, depending
who's on early shift)
wet backstreets hushed
at 2am, so quiet each
footstep echoes, fades,
our sound and shape
dissolved in rain.

ACKNOWLEDGMENTS

are due to *Dream Catcher*, *The Egg Box*, *Flirtation* (The Joy of Six anthology), *Litter* (www.leafepress.com), *Revolt*, *Seam*, *Tabourey*, *The Reater*, www.LondonArt.co.uk, and in the USA, *Pearl* and *Rattapallax*.

'Blood & Sand' won a prize in the 2002 Bridport competition. Along with 'Affinity' it also appeared in the pamphlet *Natural Causes* (Shoestring Press, 2003). 'Alaska' was a prizewinner in the Kent & Sussex competition 2002.

The author is grateful to Arts Council England for a grant supporting the completion of this book. Special thanks to Dan Thomas, Dan Hodiern, Pete Willcock, Ben Cooper, James Stoddart, Perry Haldenby, Giles Fry, Ashley Moore and all the other barmen. The following were also consulted:

Booth's Handbook of Cocktails & Mixed Drinks (Pan Books, 1966)
Cocktails & Mixed Drinks by Charles A Tuck (Kaye & Ward, 1967)
International Guide to Drinks (Hutchinson, 1976)
Michael Jackson's Bar & Cocktail Book (Mitchell Beazley, 1995)
Classic 1000 Cocktails (Foulsham, 1996)
Sauceguide to Drink and Drinking (Sauce Guides, 2001)
www.schweppeseuro.com

Dream Song, Paul Mariani's biography of John Berryman
(University of Massachusetts Press, 1996)
The Broken Tower, a biography of Hart Crane by the same author
(Norton, 1999)
A Life of Dylan Thomas by Paul Ferris
(Phoenix, 2000)

Aisle16
Live From the Hellfire Club

'Poetry has come of age.'
The Guardian

'They do with words what
I try to do with art.'
Ralph Steadman

newwriting.net

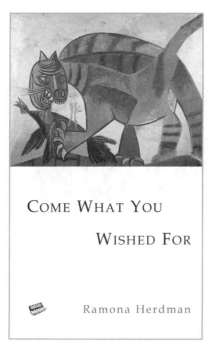

COME WHAT YOU

WISHED FOR

Ramona Herdman

Ramona Herdman
Come What You Wished For

'New poetry at its
sparkling, thrilling best.'
Julia Bell

'Life affirming.'
Catherine Smith

newwriting.net

**Richard Evans
The Zoo Keeper**

'Poetry as it should be, red in
tooth and claw.'
Concrete

'Buy this.'
Martin Newell, The Independent

newwriting.net